Dark Emperor
& Other Poems of the Night

Written by Joyce Sidman Illustrated by Rick Allen

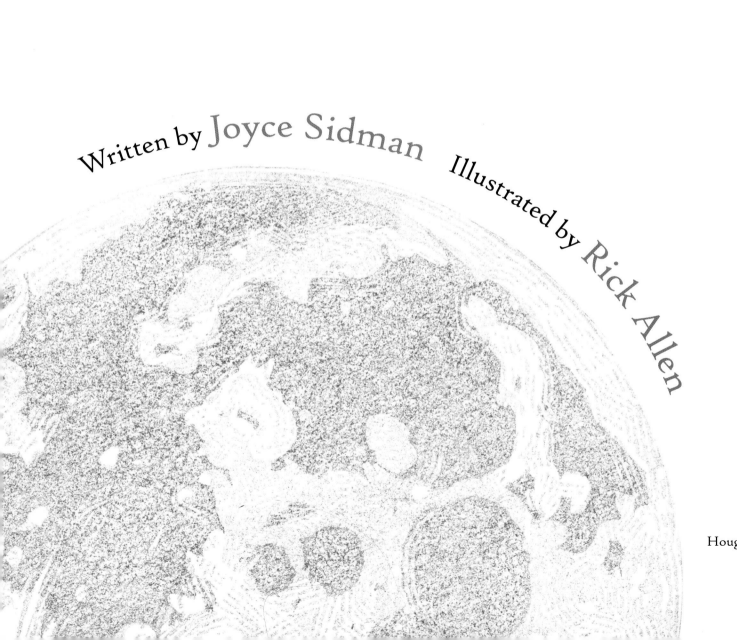

Houghton Mifflin Books for Children
Houghton Mifflin Harcourt
Boston New York 2010

To Gabe, my brave woodsman, who knows the night. —J.S.

For Herself, and those other few too dear to name. —R.N.A.

Text copyright © 2010 by Joyce Sidman
Illustrations copyright © 2010 by Rick Allen

The artist wishes to acknowledge our Kenspeckle assistant and colleague Janelle Miller,
without whose invaluable help he might still be staring at a pile of blank blocks in irresolute despair.

Houghton Mifflin Books for Children is an imprint of Houghton Mifflin Harcourt Publishing Company.

www.hmhbooks.com

The text of this book is set in Hightower and The Sans.
The prints in this book were made by the process of relief printing. A drawing or sketch is transferred onto a block of wood or,
in this instance, a sheet of linoleum mounted on wood, and the drawing is then cut and carved away using a variety of tools.
The areas left uncut are covered with ink and printed on paper by hand or on a press; a number of blocks can be cut and then
successively printed in different colors, with the different blocks being "registered" or aligned to create a multicolored print.
The prints for *Dark Emperor* were each printed from at least three blocks (and in some instances as many as six) and then hand-
colored with a strongly pigmented watercolor called gouache. There are definitely faster methods of making a picture,
but few more enjoyable in a backwards sort of way.

Library of Congress Cataloging-in-Publication Data
Sidman, Joyce.
Dark emperor and other poems of the night / written by Joyce Sidman ; illustrated by Rick Allen.
p. cm.   ISBN 978-0-547-15228-8
1. Night—Juvenile poetry. 2. Children's poetry, American. I. Title.
PS3569.I295D37 2010   811'.54—dc22   2009049696

Manufactured in Singapore
TWP 10 9 8 7 6 5 4 3 2 1
4500220973

Contents

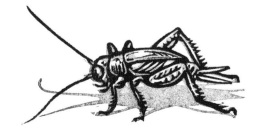

Welcome to the Night

To all of you who crawl and creep,
who buzz and chirp and hoot and peep,
who wake at dusk and throw off sleep:
Welcome to the night.

To you who make the forest sing,
who dip and dodge on silent wing,
who flutter, hover, clasp, and cling:
Welcome to the night!

Come feel the cool and shadowed breeze,
come smell your way among the trees,
come touch rough bark and leathered leaves:
Welcome to the night.

The night's a sea of dappled dark,
the night's a feast of sound and spark,
the night's a wild, enchanted park.
Welcome to the night!

As night falls, the nocturnal world wakes. Mice begin to stir, moths flutter into the starlight, and deer step out from hidden places to roam and forage. Having rested all day in a hollow tree, the **raccoon** lumbers down at dusk to search for food. Curious, intelligent, and omnivorous, the raccoon has nimble front paws that are good for digging, climbing, and prying open almost anything. Its well-developed sense of touch—almost unparalleled in the mammal world—serves it well in the darkness. Making its unhurried way across the forest, the raccoon forages by feel—inside a log (for insects), down a hole (for eggs), even underwater (for frogs or crayfish).

Snail at Moonrise

Each night, Snail
unhooks himself from earth,
climbs a slick trail of silver
up, up
the horizon of log,
up stems of leaves
to their dewy tips,
seeking
with his tiny sandpaper tongue
morsels of green
to mix in his dark, moist body
and spin
into whorls of light.

Shell-maker
Moon-maker
gleaming silver-bright.
Each night:
darkness
      into
         light.

Night is cooler, wetter, and (in some ways) safer for many animals. Woodland **snails,** for example, have moist, sluglike bodies that are in constant danger of drying out. During the day, they hide in damp places under logs and stones, but at night they emerge to search for food, riding on a cushion of slime, which protects them from sharp objects. They do not chew, but rather scrape plant material into their mouths with a tongue that is covered by rows of tiny teeth. Young snails add a layer to their shells each night. While they feed, their bodies produce a special material that hardens at the lip of the shell, extending and widening its perfectly spiral shape.

9

Love Poem of the Primrose Moth

Evening unfolds like a primrose,
pale and scented.

The moon, a primrose:
two faces glowing.

Which is sweeter: night flight
or the nectar of a primrose?

I have only one true love:
it is the primrose.

At dawn, I fold my sherbet-colored wings
and become

       a primrose.

Since it's difficult to see in the dark, night creatures use other senses to move through their world: smell, touch, hearing— even taste. The plumelike antennae of night-flying **moths** actually "smell" the air, guiding moths to both mates and food. The dainty primrose moth— barely half an inch long—is drawn to the smell of one particular flower: the evening primrose, the petals of which open at dusk. Primrose moth caterpillars feed only on evening primrose leaves, and adult moths stay near this night-blooming flower, sipping its nectar and pollinating it in the process. During the day, they cling to its stems, perfectly camouflaged: the exact rosy-yellow color of an evening primrose bud.

Dark Emperor

Perched   missile,
    almost invisible, you
        preen silent feathers,
        swivel your sleek satellite
    dish of head. What fills the
cool moons of your mesmerizing
    eyes? What waves of sound
        funnel toward those waiting
    ears? What symphonies of
        squeaks and skitters, darts
        and rustles, swell the vast,
    breathing darkness of your
        realm? O Dark Emperor
        of hooked face and
    hungry eye: turn that
        awful beak away
            from me;
            disregard

the tiny hiccup
of my heart
as I flee.

Nocturnal animals have specially adapted senses for hunting. Whereas raccoons use extrasensitive paws to feel for prey, great horned **owls** have huge eyes and extraordinary hearing; their wide, flat faces channel sound toward two large ear cavities on the sides of their head. They can also swivel their head more than halfway in either direction, although not all the way around. As night falls, the great horned owl moves from its deep-woods roost to a high perch near the forest's edge. With eyes and ears a hundred times more sensitive than a human's, it scouts for anything from salamanders to mice to rabbits. Like other owls', its feathers are soft-edged, so it can fly silently and pounce without warning on unsuspecting prey.

13

Oak After Dark

As nighttime rustles at my knee,
I stand in silent gravity

and quietly continue chores
of feeding leaves and sealing pores.

While beetles whisper in my bark,
while warblers roost in branches dark,

I stretch my roots into the hill
and slowly, slowly, drink my fill.

A thousand crickets scream my name,
yet I remain the same, the same.

I do not rest, I do not sleep,
and all my promises I keep:

to stand while all the seasons fly,
to anchor earth,
            to touch the sky.

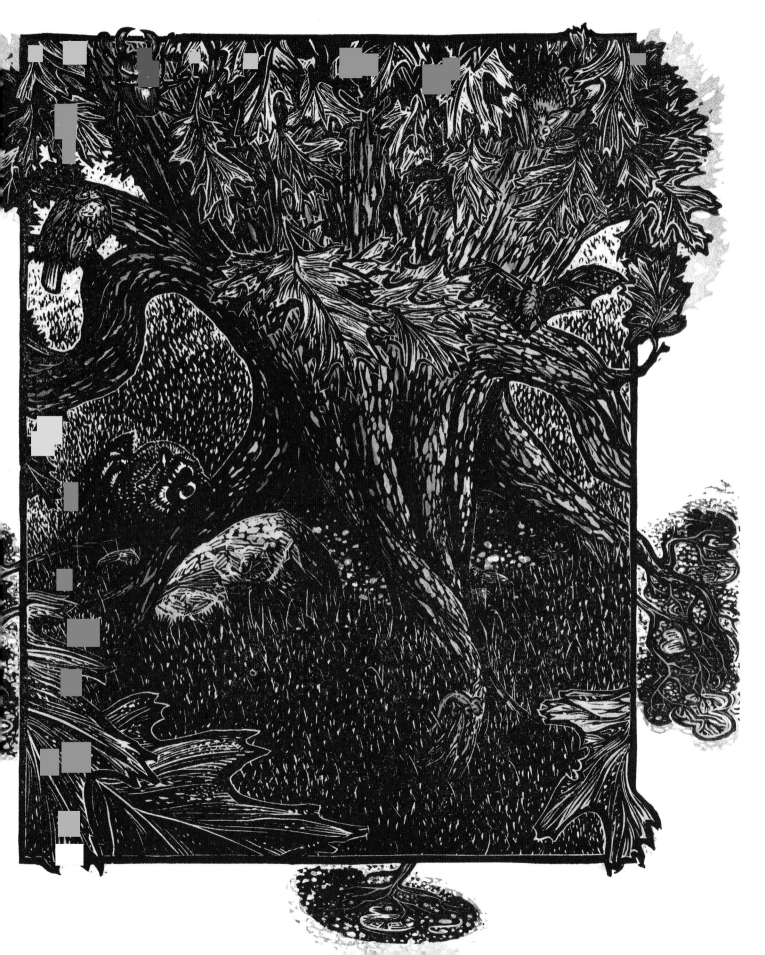

Although they don't look it, **trees**—like most plants—are constantly busy. All day, they change sunlight into food through a process called photosynthesis. They grow new branches, and give off oxygen and moisture. Their leaves are nibbled, twigs broken, and bark attacked by insects and fungi. Nighttime—when food production shuts down—is the time for recovery and repair. The roots of oaks and other trees take in extra water at night to make up for daytime's loss, and distribute it—along with food the leaves have made—through a complex system of "veins." Trees also grow new roots at night, and repair themselves by sealing off wound sites and strengthening newly formed leaves.

Night-Spider's Advice

Build a frame
and stick to it,
I always say.
Life's a circle.
Just keep going around.
Do your work, then
sit back and see
what falls in your lap.
Eat your triumphs,
eat your mistakes:
that way your belly
will always be full.
Use what you have.
Rest when you need to.
Dawn will come soon enough.
Someone has to remake
the world each night.
It might as well be you.

Many insects are busy after dark: hunting for food, attracting mates, or laying eggs. Some **spiders** are nocturnal, too. The orb spider builds a new spiral-shaped web each night, often in the same spot and using the same anchor threads. Web silk—an incredibly strong, elastic thread—is formed as a liquid inside the spider's body and pulled out from six "spinnerets" in its abdomen. Each spinneret produces a different kind of silk: some strong, some silky, some for making egg sacs. When web-making, the spider first lays down spoke threads, which will serve as walkways. Then it weaves a spiral of sticky silk to snag night insects such as flies, moths, and mosquitoes. Toward dawn, after a night of hunting, most orb spiders eat their damaged webs, which provide nutrients for a fresh batch of silk.

17

I Am a Baby Porcupette

I am a baby porcupette.
My paws are small; my nose is wet.
And as I nurse against my mom,
we mew and coo a soft duet.

I am a baby porcupette.
I cannot climb up branches yet.
While Mom sleeps in the trees, I curl
beneath a log till sun has set.

I am a baby porcupette.
I nibble in the nighttime wet:
a sprig of leaves, a tuft of grass,
in hidden spots I won't forget.

I am a baby porcupette.
My fur is soft; my eyes are jet.
But I can deal with any threat:
I raise my quills
         and pirouette.

Nocturnal animal babies must learn the ways of the night from their parents in order to survive. A baby **porcupine**—called a porcupette—spends the day hidden under a stone or log while its mother sleeps on a branch above. When evening falls, the mother comes down to greet her baby, and the two "sing" to each other while the porcupette nurses. As the mother forages, she leads her baby to delicacies such as raspberry leaves or tender twigs. The porcupette also practices climbing on small logs, to prepare for a life in the trees. If danger approaches, he instinctively whirls around and lashes out with a tail already filled with quills. Within four months, the porcupette has become a full-grown porcupine, ready to wander the nighttime woods on his own.

19

Cricket Speaks

All day
I wandered through
the quiet,
napping and gnawing.
Waiting for the
first chirp,
the quickening voices,
the raucous scrape
of wing against wing.

Now
it is midnight,
the trilling hour,
and all I want
is to feel the thick heat
on the hard case of my body
and sing,

      sing,

till the branches tremble
and life
      swells
to a single
      searing,
        unstoppable
          sound.

Night in the woods is noisy. Tree frogs chirp, owls hoot, and bears rustle through the underbrush. One of the loudest and longest-lasting sounds is the call of the male **cricket.** Crickets' wings are not for flying, but rather for making music. One wing has a "file"— with serrated teeth like a comb—which is rubbed against a hard "scraper" on the other wing to attract a mate. The resulting sound is called stridulation, and in the late summer and early autumn, it can swell to deafening levels— peaking at about midnight, then diminishing toward morning. Amazingly, female crickets (who don't stridulate, but make only soft sounds) have the ability to pick out a mate from all those calls, based on the length and strength of his song. Crickets are more active in warm weather; in fact, in 1897, a scientist named A. E. Dolbear worked out a formula to calcu-late outside temperature based on how fast a tree cricket trills!

The Mushrooms Come

From moss and loam
the mushrooms come.

From bark on trees,
from crumbling logs,
from musty leaves,
the mushrooms come.

From vast pale networks
underground
they shoulder up
without a sound;
they spread their damp
umbrella tops
and loose their spores
with silent pops.
Unbuttoning the forest floor,
the mushrooms come,
the mushrooms come.

Like noses pink
in midnight air,
like giants' ears,
like elfin hair,
like ancient cities
built on cliffs,
the mushrooms come,
the mushrooms come.

Mushrooms are not plants; they belong to their own kingdom, Fungi. Plants need sunlight to grow and make energy, but mushrooms do not—they live on decaying matter such as rotting logs, stumps, and leaves. They grow beneath the surface in a tangled mass of rootlike hairs. When temperature and moisture conditions are just right—often at night—some of these "hairs" begin to swell and push their way out of soil or bark, appearing as the visible part of a mushroom. One mushroom can produce up to two billion spores (reproductive cells), which pop from the closely packed gills beneath the mushroom's cap and drift out over the forest floor. Mushrooms provide food for insects and animals alike, and many have fantastical names based on their appearance, such as tree ears, worm coral, and inky cap. Some—like the death cap or destroying angel—are poisonous to humans.

23

Ballad of the Wandering Eft

Come all you young efts,
so brave and so bold,
and don the bright colors
of scarlet and gold.

Step out from your puddles
to breathe the sweet air
and wander the woodlands
with hardly a care.

For it's wild and it's windy
way out in the woods,
where the moss grows like candy
and the hunting is good,
where the rain falls from heaven
and mud's underfoot.
It's wild and it's windy
way out in the woods.

In the moonlight you'll journey;
through the day you will roam;

you'll crawl over tree roots
and wade through the loam.

You'll rove till you're weary,
then return to the pond,
where you'll dream of your life
as an eft vagabond.

For it's wild and it's windy
way out in the woods,
where the moss grows like candy
and the hunting is good,
where the rain falls from heaven
and mud's underfoot.
It's wild and it's windy
way out in the woods.

Some woodland creatures are active both day and night. Red **efts**—like other newts and salamanders—must keep their skin moist to survive, so they roam mostly at night when it is damp. But often, after a summer rain, efts will venture into the wet daytime woods to hunt small grubs and insects. Their bright orange-red color protects them; it warns predators (such as bullfrogs or raccoons) of the toxic chemicals in their skin. Red efts are actually the land-dwelling stage of the red-spotted newt. Newts are born in the water, and, after two to four years as a land-roving eft, they fade to an olive green color, return to the water, and grow gills once again. Their roaming days are over.

Bat Wraps Up

Belly full,
he drops down
from the echoing room of night.
One last swift swoop,
one last bug plucked from air
with cupped tail,
scooped neatly to mouth.

As dark grows thin
and body heavy,
he tumbles to tree
and grasps bark,
folds that swirl of cape
tipped with tiny claws
and snags the spot
that smells like home.

Then . . . upside flip,
lock-on grip . . .
stretch, hang, relax.
Yawn . . .

        dawn.

As night ends, nocturnal creatures must find hidden or camouflaged places to rest to avoid daytime predators. Raccoons climb back to their tree roosts, spiders hide beneath leaves, and snails creep back under logs. Tree **bats** have spent all night on the wing, hunting for moths, mosquitoes, and other insects. Bats are mammals, and their wings are actually "hands" with elongated webbed fingers. To locate insects as they fly, they use a process called echolocation; their sensitive ears pick up the echoes of their own high-pitched cries, allowing them to "see" objects in the dark. They quickly scoop up insects in their tail membranes and flip them into their mouths. As day approaches, tree bats look for a branch or loose piece of bark to roost under. Hanging upside down by their feet, wings folded, they look like nothing more than a dead leaf swaying in the morning breeze.

Moon's Lament (an ubi sunt)

Where are the bright dips of fireflies?

Where are the zigzags of moths?

Where are the diving sweeps of the nighthawk

and where its haunting cry?

Where is the thrum of crickets,

the throbbing of frogs?

Where are the great flocks of travelers

whose soft wings whispered to me,

wave upon wave,

beating toward some distant wood?

Where are the stars?

Where are the pale scarves of clouds?

Where are my ghostly shadows,

my pools of molten silver,

poured with such extravagance?

Where has it all gone—

my glory,

my radiance—

now that day has come?

Alas. Another eternity of sunbeams to wait.

The **moon** does not make its own light; it is like a big mirror, reflecting the sun's rays. When we can see all of the sunbathed part of the moon, we call it "full." A full moon rises at sunset, shines all night, and sets at dawn. But when the moon is waxing or waning, it is often out in the daylight: a pale white shape in the daytime sky. During spring and fall, huge flocks of songbirds migrate at night, using the moon and stars to help them navigate thousands of miles to and from their summer breeding grounds. They fly at night to avoid daytime predators and to take advantage of the cool, calm air. As the day approaches and the moon fades, these flocks settle down to rest and eat.

Glossary

abdomen In spiders, the hindmost (and usually the largest) part of the body.

antennae (singular, *antenna*) A pair of flexible stalks on an insect's head that are used for smell or touch.

camouflage Coloring or body parts that help animals and plants blend into the background and hide.

echolocation A method of locating objects by bouncing high-pitched sounds against them, used by such animals as bats and dolphins.

fungi (singular, *fungus*) A group of spore-making organisms that feed on decaying organic matter.

migrate In birds, to move from one region to another in order to raise young more successfully.

nectar A sugary liquid made by plants to attract pollinators such as moths and bees.

nocturnal Active at night.

omnivorous Eating a wide variety of foods, both plant and animal.

orbit To travel around a larger planet or star in a circular path.

photosynthesis The chemical process by which plants make energy from sunlight.

pollinate To carry pollen from one flower to another, thus fertilizing the plants and allowing seeds to form.

predator An animal that hunts other animals for food.

reproductive Referring to the way an organism makes another one of itself.

spinnerets Organs in a spider's body that make and squirt out silk.

spore A tiny seedlike cell that can grow into a new organism (as in fungi).

stridulation The shrill sound made by certain insects that rub two body parts together.

ubi sunt The name of a style of medieval poetry that laments the loss of heroic, beautiful things.

wane To grow smaller.

wax To grow larger.